EXPLORER BOOKS

THE
TITANIC

by Richard Wormser

A TRUMPET CLUB ORIGINAL BOOK

Published by The Trumpet Club, Inc.,
a subsidiary of Bantam Doubleday Dell Publishing Group, Inc.,
1540 Broadway, New York, New York 10036

ISBN 0-440-83113-X

Printed in the United States of America
November 1994
3   5   7   9   10   8   6   4   2
CWO

PHOTOGRAPH CREDITS

Cover: Steven James Petruccio/Evelyne Johnson Associates.
pp. 4 & 5: Ulster Folk & Transport Museum/Harland & Wolff Collection.
pp. 10, 11, 20, & 30: Courtesy of the Mariners' Museum, Newport News, Virginia.
pp. 13, 40, & 42: © Culver Pictures.   *pp. 16 & 32:* © Camera Press/Globe Photos.
pp. 48, 52, & 56: © Woods Hole Oceanographic Institution.

Contents

Introduction

The night of April 14, 1912, was bitter cold. The sky was clear and bright with stars. The ocean was calm. The R.M.S. *Titanic,* the largest and most luxurious cruise ship of its time, was making its first voyage across the Atlantic Ocean from England to the United States. On board were approximately 1,300 passengers and 900 crew members, all thrilled to be sailing on this great ship. Little did they know what lay ahead for them: not a safe harbor in America, but a huge iceberg in the middle of the ocean. The *Titanic* would crash into the iceberg and sink to the bottom of the sea.

For 74 years, people thought about finding the great ship and raising her to the surface. Relatives of the dead, inventors, and scientists were interested, though none of them succeeded. But a marine geologist named Dr. Robert Ballard had a dream—he wanted to find the *Titanic* and discover her secrets. In 1985, he sailed to the very spot where the *Titanic* met its fate. For Ballard, it was the adventure of a lifetime. At last he found the answers to his questions —12,500 feet beneath the sea.

What happened aboard the *Titanic* the night of April 14, 1912? What did the passengers and crew do when they discovered they were in trouble? How did such a great ship sink? And what did Dr. Ballard discover lying at the bottom of the ocean?

In this book you will learn all about the great ship that sailed out into the Atlantic on its very first voyage—never to return.

1

The Unsinkable Ship

The year was 1910. The place was the Queen's Island shipyards in Belfast, Ireland. There, 14,000 workers hired by the shipbuilding company of Harland & Wolff were building a new ship for the White Star Line. The ship was named the *Titanic*.

The ship had been named after the Titans, a race of gods in ancient Greek mythology. The Titans wanted to overthrow Zeus, the king of the gods. Zeus destroyed them for their rebellion. Because of this legend, there were people who thought the name *Titanic* might bring bad luck to the ship. Other people pointed out that 12 years earlier a writer named Morgan Robertson had written a book about an imaginary ship crossing the Atlantic. This ship was said to be the biggest and most modern in the world. Yet on a cold April night, according to the book, the ship struck an iceberg and sank to the bottom of the ocean. Almost everyone aboard drowned because there weren't enough lifeboats. Robertson called his ship the *Titan*.

But the builders of the *Titanic* said it was ridiculous to compare a real, modern ship like the *Titanic* to the make-believe *Titan*. They insisted that the *Titanic* was unsinkable. Anyone who thought it could sink didn't know the first thing about ships—or else had a wild imagination. Strangely enough, many of the characters in Robertson's novel had said the very same thing before the *Titan* sank.

3

The Titanic *was built in 1910 at the Queen's Island shipyards in Belfast, Ireland.*

The shipbuilders did have a point. The *Titanic* was the largest ship of its time. It was more than 880 feet—or one-sixth of a mile—long and 92 feet across at its widest point. From the *keel,* or bottom of the ship, to the *bridge,* the enclosed platform on the front upper deck where the captain and officers kept watch, the *Titanic* was more than 100 feet high—taller than a 10-story building. And it weighed 46,328 tons! The *Titanic* was powered by three propellers and had 29 boilers to provide steam power to drive the ship. The coal it used for fuel was heated in 159 furnaces. It had four huge *funnels,* or smokestacks, each wide enough for two trains to pass through at the same time.

The *Titanic* was also the most expensive ship of its day. It cost $7.5 million to build. With today's money, it would cost about $70 million to build the same ship!

The *Titanic* could reach a speed of 24 knots, or 27.6 miles, per hour. (A *knot,* the measure of a ship's speed, is slightly longer than a mile.) Today, ocean liners travel at about 30 knots.

The *Titanic* was designed by William James, an Irish nobleman. James was an excellent engineer who had designed many ships. He took great pride in building a vessel he believed would be almost unsinkable—but he made one fatal mistake.

Deadly Errors

James did not design the *Titanic*'s bulkheads high enough for such a large ship. *Bulkheads* are empty, box-like steel compartments that divide the ship into sections to prevent it from sinking. Any water that breaks through

It took 20 horses to pull this 15¹/₂-ton anchor to the Olympia, *the sister ship of the* Titanic. *The* Titanic *had an anchor just like it.*

5

the ship's sides gets trapped in the bulkheads instead of spreading throughout the ship. If the bulkheads don't trap the water, the ship will fill up and eventually sink.

Bulkheads normally reach from the bottom of the ship to the main deck above. But William James didn't think it was necessary to build them so high. He designed the *Titanic*'s bulkheads to stop two decks below the main deck. Because the ship was so huge and the bulkheads were so large, he couldn't imagine them filling with water before the damage could be sealed off. The owners of the ship agreed with his decision. It meant they could use the extra space to build first-class rooms. With more rooms, the ship could travel with more passengers on board.

The builders also were careless about the number of lifeboats on board the ship. The *Titanic* carried only 16 of them, each of which could hold approximately 60 passengers. A ship carrying 2,200 people should have had at least 40 lifeboats.

According to the regulations for English ships set by the British Board of Trade, no ship had to carry more than 16 lifeboats. For most ships, that was more than enough. But the law had been passed years earlier, before anyone imagined that there would ever be a ship as large as the *Titanic*.

The builders knew the law was outdated and needed to be changed. But they also knew that adding more lifeboats would leave less space for passengers—and with fewer rooms on board, profits for the owners would be smaller. As a compromise, they agreed to add four smaller-size lifeboats. Even that was not enough. The *Titanic* could carry a maximum of 3,943 passengers and crew, and there would be enough lifeboats for about 1,178 people. Should the ship sink, more than two-thirds of the people on board could drown.

Of course, the builders and the owners honestly believed

that they didn't need to take the usual safety precautions with the *Titanic*. The ship was so large, so well built, and so modern that it was hard to imagine it sinking.

The Greatest Ship Ever Built

The owners of the *Titanic* were determined to build the best ship that ever sailed the ocean. So they made the *Titanic* into a floating palace. No expense was spared to make her the most luxurious ship in the world. The finest materials were used in her construction, and the best workmen were hired. The orders were to build the *Titanic* for "comfort rather than speed." At the same time, the White Star Line also ordered the building of a sister ship, the *Olympia*. The two ships were similar in many ways, but the *Titanic* was fancier.

Work on the *Titanic* began in 1909. Two years later, on May 11, 1911, a hundred thousand cheering people gathered at the Belfast docks to watch the launching of the *Titanic*. It took 22 tons of soap, oil, and grease to slide the ship off the ramp on which it had been built and into the water. But the *Titanic* wasn't finished yet. All the interior work and painting still had to be done.

The best craftsmen from England and Ireland came to decorate the passenger areas. Throughout the summer of 1911, they prepared the *Titanic* for her *maiden,* or first, voyage. They installed her plumbing, electricity, cooling, and water systems. Then they built and furnished her cabins and dining rooms, restaurants and concert halls, decks and berths, and swimming pools and gymnasiums. They also installed 4 elevators and a switchboard with 50 telephone lines for calls within the ship. In addition, the *Titanic* was outfitted with a new invention called the *wireless,* a communications system for sending radio signals to other ships at sea.

In mid-September, the date for the *Titanic*'s maiden voy-

7

age was announced: March 20, 1912. Two days later, the first of a series of events took place that would lead up to the tragedy that lay ahead. The *Titanic*'s sister ship, the *Olympia,* collided with another vessel and needed repairs. As a result, the completion of the *Titanic* was delayed. A new sailing date—April 10, 1912—was announced.

2

On Board the *Titanic*

Captain Edward J. Smith stood proudly on the deck of the magnificent *Titanic* as tugboats pulled it away from the Belfast dock and out to sea. No one had ever commanded such a huge ship before. Cheering crowds lined the Irish coast to catch sight of the great ship and her famous captain.

It was April 2, 1912, eight days before the *Titanic* was set to sail on her seven-day voyage to New York. But before the *Titanic* could take on passengers, she had to pass a trial run at sea.

Captain Smith put the *Titanic* through a series of tests. For 570 miles he stopped and started the ship, turned her around in a circle, and wove a snake-like path through the water. He pushed her close to full speed, then suddenly stopped or reversed engines. Everything went better than expected, and the *Titanic* was declared fit to sail.

Because no one had ever commanded a ship that large, some people thought the captain should have made even more tests before sailing out to sea. Did he really know how long it would take the ship to stop when running at full speed? Did he know how long it would take the ship to turn away from a dangerous object in the water? The answer to these and other questions was no. But there was no time for him to find out. The *Titanic* was scheduled to sail in just over a week.

The Cabins

After the trial runs, the huge ship sailed for Southampton, England, where it would prepare for its maiden voyage and take on some passengers. There were a total of 1,320 passengers registered for the trip, less than half the number that the ship could accommodate. The passenger sections of the ship were divided into three main areas: first-, second-, and third-class.

The first-class passengers paid the highest fares and got the best rooms. A first-class cabin cost anywhere from $1,500 to $4,500, depending upon its size and location. (Only the very rich could afford these cabins.) Second-class passengers paid $65 and higher for much simpler cabins. And third-class passengers paid $36.25 and had the simplest cabins of all. Each class had its own deck space, res-

The first-class grand staircase of the Titanic *was photographed before the ship set sail.*

taurant areas, lounges, smoking rooms, bars, decks, and recreational facilities. Passengers in one class were strictly prohibited from visiting a higher-class area.

The *Titanic*'s first-class cabins were the most elegant of any ship of its day, with expensive wood paneling and antique furniture. The linens and towels were of the best quality. The largest cabins contained three rooms—a bedroom, sitting room, and servants' room. Many wealthy people traveled with one or more servants and wanted their servants' quarters nearby.

First-class cabins were located on the upper level of the vessel. There, passengers were less likely to feel the rocking motion of the ship that causes some people to become seasick. The first-class area contained several elegant restaurants, a concert hall, a library, sunrooms, a gymna-

Men spent many hours in the first-class smoking room on the Titanic. *In those days, women were not allowed to smoke in public.*

sium, swimming pool, French-style cafe, miniature golf course, winter garden, and smoking room. In those days, gentlemen didn't smoke in the presence of ladies. And ladies were not supposed to smoke at all: Those who did had to do so in private.

The second-class cabins were smaller and simpler than those in first class. The recreational and dining rooms were comfortable but not fancy. Even so, many passengers considered second class on the *Titanic* to be far better than first class on other ships.

The third-class rooms were small, neat, and rather bare. Some held as many as six people. The dining room was plain and simple, and so were the meals. There were bars and smoking rooms, as well as a large public room where people could sit and talk or read. The worst thing about third class was its location—in the lower part of the ship, where the motion of the vessel was most obvious. As a result, many third-class passengers suffered from seasickness—especially during rough weather.

The Passengers

First class, with 337 people on board, was about half full. Someone said that if the fortunes of the first-class passengers were added together, they would total $500 million. Only 271 passengers bought second-class tickets, less than half of those available. But third class, with 712 passengers, was nearly full. Most of these travelers were immigrants with large families. They came from Finland, Ireland, the Middle East, England, China, India, France, and Germany.

Before sailing for the United States, the *Titanic* took on passengers in three different countries—England, France, and Ireland.

The boarding of the first-class passengers was a major social event in each of the ports. Some of the richest and most famous people in the world were making the voyage. Among them were John Jacob Astor and his new bride, Madeline. Mr. Astor was considered to be the wealthiest man in America, with a fortune somewhere between $75 million and $100 million. That fortune would be worth more than a billion dollars today.

Astor wasn't the only millionaire on board. There was also Charles Guggenheim, whose family owned copper mines all over the world. Other wealthy passengers included Ida and Isidor Straus, who founded Macy's department store; Bruce Ismay, chairman of the White Star Line, which owned the *Titanic;* and Thomas Andrews, one of the company's chief engineers.

The rich did not travel lightly. Mrs. Charlotte Cardeza of Philadelphia came with 14 trunks, 4 suitcases, 3 crates, and a medicine chest. Her luggage contained, among other things, 70 dresses, 10 fur coats, and 91 pairs of gloves. Another passenger, William Carter, brought along 60

John Jacob Astor, thought to be the wealthiest man in America at the time, sailed on the Titanic *with Madeline, his new bride.*

shirts, 15 pairs of shoes, 2 tuxedos, 24 polo sticks—and even his Renault car!

In those days, wealthy people in society were expected to change clothes several times a day. They wore one outfit for breakfast and a different one for lunch. Then there were special clothes to play in and special clothes to lounge in. Every afternoon, tea was served, and that meant yet another change of clothes. In the evening, everyone dressed up for dinner—the women in formal gowns and the men in tuxedos. And nobody wanted to be seen wearing the same outfit twice during the same voyage.

Among the well-dressed first-class passengers were two unusual men who called themselves "Boy" Bradley and "Kid" Homer. These men were professional gamblers who had come to play cards with the wealthy—and cheat them out of their money. There was also a mysterious man traveling with two children. He gave his name as Hoffman. It was later discovered that his real name was Michael Navratil, and that after being separated from his wife, he had kidnapped the children.

Some first-class passengers brought their pets on board, too. John Jacob Astor had his Airedale, named Kitty. And Henry Harper of the Boston publishing family brought his prize Pekingese, Sun Yat Sen, named after the president of China. One woman even brought some prize roosters with her, but she was not allowed to keep them in her cabin. They were held below the main decks.

Most of the second-class passengers were middle-class people on vacation or traveling to America on business. Among them were a number of artists, writers, ministers, and teachers. There were also some young honeymooners.

Because of a coal strike in England, several other White Line ships scheduled to leave for the United States had been forced to cancel their voyages. As a result, many passengers were transferred from those ships to the second-class area on the *Titanic*. Most considered themselves lucky to be on such a magnificent ship.

The third-class passengers were mostly emigrants from Europe and the Middle East, who were traveling with large families. Many of them were dressed in the clothes and costumes of their native countries. They spoke a variety of languages, and during the voyage they would often play music and sing songs from their homelands. Some were traveling to America to seek their fortune, some to join their families who had already settled there. But all of them were excited about beginning a new life in a new land.

The Crew

The *Titanic* had 900 crew members on board. They were divided into two main groups—those who ran the ship and those who provided service to the passengers.

Captain Edward J. Smith, known as E. J. to his friends, was in charge of the ship. He was 62 years old and had spent more than 40 years at sea. He was an extremely popular man with both the crew and passengers. Smith had commanded many ships but none as large as the *Titanic*. One observer had called the ship "a monster," and doubted whether anybody could really control such a huge vessel. But Smith was thought to be an excellent sea captain, and there was no doubt among the owners that he was the right man for the job.

Captain Smith was assisted by a number of chief officers, and first-, second-, third-, fourth-, and fifth-officers. The lowest ranking members of the crew were those who performed physical labor deep in the bottom of the ship. Their job was to keep the engines running smoothly and make sure there was enough heat in the boilers to supply power.

Edward J. Smith was captain of the Titanic.

The stokers, firemen, and trimmers took care of the boilers and furnaces; greasers oiled machinery; and engineers supplied electrical power to the ship. Not only was their work physically hard, but it was carried out in the hottest areas of the ship. These men almost never spoke with passengers, since passengers rarely went below the main decks.

Two of the most important jobs belonged to the lookouts and the radio operators. Lookouts climbed high up the ship's mast to the *crow's nest,* a basket large enough for two men. From the crow's nest they could see far out over the ocean. Their job was to keep watch for anything floating in the water, such as wreckage or icebergs, that could collide with the *Titanic.* The radio operator's job was to communicate with other radio operators, both on sea and on land. In 1912, ships were just beginning to use radio waves to communicate. Before that, they used large blinking lights to send messages in Morse code. But a blinking light could be seen only a few miles away. Radio waves could be picked up from almost 1,000 miles away.

When it came to providing services for the passengers, the number-one job was that of steward or stewardess, especially in first class. Each steward was assigned a certain number of cabins and worked either a day or night shift. A first-class steward might have as few as eight cabins to service, while second-class stewards often had up to 20. Stewards were responsible for the well-being of everyone in their cabins. A number of other workers performed specialized jobs for passengers. Included in this group were bellboys, clothes pressers, doctors and hospital attendants, post-office workers, gym instructors, janitors, waiters, and cooks. There were also eight musicians on board who entertained the passengers.

Supplies

It would take a lot of food to feed more than 2,000 passengers and crew for 7 days. The shopping list included hundreds of thousands of pounds of food and beverages:

Fresh meat	*75,000 pounds*
Fresh fish	*11,000 pounds*
Bacon and ham	*7,500 pounds*
Poultry and game (some live)	*25,000 pounds*
Fresh eggs	*40,000*
Ice cream	*1,750 quarts*
Coffee	*2,200 pounds*
Sugar	*10,000 pounds*
Cereals	*10,000 boxes*
Oranges	*36,000*

Fresh milk	*1,500 gallons*
Fresh butter	*6,000 pounds*
Onions	*3,500 pounds*
Jams and Marmalades	*1,120 jars*
Beer	*20,000 bottles*
Wines	*1,500 bottles*
Mineral water	*15,000 bottles*

The following items were needed for the dining rooms and cabins:

Breakfast cups	*4,500*
Coffee cups	*1,500*
Dinner plates	*12,000*
Soup plates	*4,500*
Dessert plates	*2,000*
Coffee pots	*1,200*
Salt shakers	*2,000*
Dinner forks	*8,000*
Teaspoons	*6,000*
Blankets	*7,500*
Sheets	*1,800*
Bath towels	*7,500*
Pillow cases	*15,000*

3

The Voyage

Shortly before noon on April 10, 1912, bells rang out in the harbor of Southampton, England. The *Titanic* joined the chorus with three long, deep blasts of its whistles—the longest and loudest in shipping history. Tugboats began leading the great ship out into the bay. Then the captain ordered the crew to start the engines, and the *Titanic* moved out under its own power. The crowds on shore cheered.

When the *Titanic* set sail, a number of passengers and crew were left behind. Several firemen who worked in the ship's boiler room had stayed too long in a bar and returned late for work. They cursed the officer who refused to let them on board. A few passengers arrived too late as well.

In addition, about 60 people had canceled their reservations. Some important businessmen—J. P. Morgan, Henry Clay Frick, and Horace Harding—changed their plans at the last minute because of business affairs or illness. Mr. and Mrs. George Vanderbilt, one of the wealthiest and most famous couples in the United States, decided not to sail because Mrs. Vanderbilt's mother didn't think it was safe to travel on a ship's maiden voyage. "So much can go wrong," she said. The Vanderbilts canceled their booking, even though their luggage had already been sent aboard.

The Titanic *set sail on her maiden voyage on April 10, 1912.*

However, one of their servants stayed on board to watch their belongings.

Ice in the Water

To the passengers on board, the ocean seemed calm and beautiful and the voyage smooth and uneventful. But seamen crossing the North Atlantic earlier that spring had seen something that worried them a lot. From a distance, the scene they saw looked like a fleet of sailing ships or a white mountain range drifting in the water. A closer look revealed a more familiar—and terrifying—sight. It was a fleet of icebergs, 78 miles long.

The icebergs had traveled from Greenland, located largely within the Arctic Circle. Greenland is an island of almost solid ice 2 miles high, formed by half a million years of falling snow. Across the land run rivers of ice, called *glaciers,* which creep forward at the rate of about 65 feet a day. When the face of a glacier reaches the bay, great slabs of ice break off and crash into the water. Eventually these slabs drift into the ocean as icebergs.

Scientists believe that sometime in 1910 one such slab broke off in Jacobhavn Bay on the west coast of Greenland. They estimate that it was 100 feet high, 300 feet long, and weighed about a million pounds. Only about 20 percent of the iceberg could be seen. The other 80 percent was hidden under water. The iceberg was almost 500 feet deep below the surface.

Carried along by ocean currents and pushed around by bitter cold winds, the iceberg would first travel north to the Arctic seas and then slowly make its way south with thousands of other icebergs. Normally, icebergs stay in these northern regions and don't reach the North Atlantic, which is farther south. But the winter of 1912 had been extremely mild and thousands of icebergs had floated southward to the sea lanes, the routes ships travel across the ocean.

Beautiful on top of the water, the icebergs were deadly below the surface. They were hard as rock, with sharp spurs extending outward. Any ship that came too close could be torn open. By April of 1912, as the *Titanic* began its journey to New York, hundreds of icebergs were drifting idly into the ship's path.

The captain and officers of the *Titanic* should have known that there was ice in their way. At least 20 ships traveling in both directions across the Atlantic had reported seeing icebergs on or near the *Titanic*'s course. Not all of those messages were sent directly to the *Titanic,* however. In fact, only six of them reached the ship as it sailed across the ocean, and only two of those were actually brought to Captain Smith's attention. Still, he and his officers knew they were headed toward icebergs even if they didn't know how serious the problem was. Yet, for some reason, no one seemed concerned enough to take any precautions, such as slowing down or having an extra lookout on duty.

By the end of her first full day on the open sea, the *Titanic* had covered only 386 miles as the captain and the crew got to know the ship. On the second day, however, the *Titanic* ran close to 22 miles an hour and covered 519 miles. She made equally good time on the third day. The captain, determined to reach New York on schedule, was keeping up the pace. He saw no reason to slow down. By the time the *Titanic* met its tragic fate, the ship was halfway to New York and had been sailing for 3½ days.

The Last Night

As the *Titanic* rapidly approached the icefield, the passengers were unaware of any danger. During the day, people walked around or sat on the deck, played cards, read, or wrote letters in the lounges. First-class passengers also played handball, swam, or worked out in the gym. The gym was equipped with stationary bicycles, mechanical horses, and a machine shaped like a camel. The gym instructor encouraged everybody to ride on it because, he claimed, it was good for the liver. Some passengers preferred to take a steam bath or get a massage.

Sunday, April 12, was a beautiful, bright, clear day. After breakfast, religious services were held throughout the ship. Although the weather had been cool up until then, it suddenly began to get very cold. People went indoors to warm themselves by fireplaces and electric heaters. The ship's officers began to measure the ocean temperature. It was rapidly becoming colder, a sign that icebergs might be nearby.

Later that evening, a group of wealthy men and women

22

arranged a private dinner party for Captain Smith. After dinner, Captain Smith met with several of his officers and talked about the difficulty of spotting icebergs on a calm, clear, moonless night with no waves in the ocean. The lookouts' job was actually made more difficult by the calmness of the water. If there had been waves, the men would have been more likely to spot an iceberg, for they might have seen the white crest of the water breaking over the ice.

The captain advised the officers to keep an extra sharp lookout, and then he went to bed. Many passengers were also preparing for bed. It was too cold to do much else. By 10:30, most people had returned to their cabins.

As the passengers were bedding down for the night, Harold Bridge, one of the radio operators, was hard at work in the radio room. He was sending a number of private messages written by the passengers to their friends and relatives on shore. Suddenly, he was interrupted by an incoming message from the freighter *Californian*. The *Californian* was trapped in an ice floe about 10 miles away from the *Titanic*. The *Californian* had stopped for the night, and her radio operator, Cyril Evans, was trying to warn the *Titanic* about icebergs.

But Bridge was way behind in his work and impatiently told Evans to get off the air. "Shut up," he wired, "I'm busy." He never bothered to deliver Evans's message to the *Titanic*'s officers. Evans then decided to shut down his radio and go to bed. Since he was the *Californian*'s only radio operator, there was no one to take his place. Until he returned to work the next morning, the *Californian* wasn't able to send or receive radio messages.

The night was bitter cold. Stars shone like diamonds in the dark sky, but there was no moon. The water was calm, and smooth as glass. High in the crow's nest, two young sailors, Frederick Fleet and Herbert Lee, were watching for icebergs. These men were the "eyes of the ship"—part

23

of the team of lookouts. From their perch above the *Titanic*'s deck, they could gaze far out into the open sea and spot any danger before it seriously threatened the ship. Radar and other electronic scanning devices had not yet been invented, so watching closely was the only way to spot objects in the water. But these lookouts didn't even have a pair of binoculars.

By 11:30 P.M., most passengers were in bed. Fleet and Lee were glad their shift would be over in another 20 minutes. They were numb with cold and their eyes hurt from the strain of trying to see in the dark. Then at 11:39 P.M., Fleet suddenly spied an object which at first seemed small but rapidly increased in size. Within seconds he realized that the *Titanic* was headed straight for an iceberg. He snatched up the telephone and rang the bridge, the officer's control center. As soon as the officer answered, Fleet cried out:

"Iceberg dead ahead!"

The great ship was about to meet her fate.

4

Collision!

It took only 37 seconds for the *Titanic* to begin its swing away from the 100-foot-high, 500-foot-deep iceberg in its path. To lookouts Fleet and Lee, that was way too long. It seemed certain that the *Titanic* would crash head-on into the mountain of ice. William Murdoch, the first officer in charge, had already given orders to change the ship's course. A ship as large as the *Titanic,* however, needed time to reposition. Fifteen seconds more and the *Titanic* would have escaped. But time was the one thing the *Titanic* didn't have.

The *Titanic* was about to crash into the iceberg when it suddenly began to swerve out of the iceberg's path. To the officers on the bridge, it seemed that their last-minute attempts to change course had worked. The ship appeared to have only lightly scraped the iceberg. But many passengers and crew below were aware that something much more serious had happened.

Strange Sounds

Four crew members relaxing in a first-class lounge heard a grinding noise from deep inside the ship. It sounded, one said, as if "a propeller had fallen off." Many first-class passengers felt a shock. To Marguerite Frolicher, a young Swiss woman, it seemed, "as if the ship were landing." Lady Duff Gordon, a dress designer married to a British nobleman, commented that it was as if "someone had run a giant finger along the side of the ship."

On the ship's lower decks, the noise was even louder. Some people in second class were awakened by the jolt. Major Arthur Godfrey Peuchen, a Canadian, thought "a heavy wave" had struck the ship. Mrs. Walter Stephenson, who had lived through the 1906 San Francisco earthquake, thought the shock felt like an earthquake tremor.

Deep within the ship, the men tending the boilers that powered the *Titanic* knew exactly what had happened. In one of the boiler rooms, a tremendous rumbling, scraping sound was heard, followed by a terrifying roar as tons of sea water came crashing into the ship. The whole left side of the ship seemed to collapse suddenly. The men barely escaped with their lives.

In the third-class area, Carl Bohme, a Finnish immigrant, got out of bed to see what was going on and found himself up to his ankles in water. In the mailroom, the water was already covering the knees of the postal workers, who were frantically trying to keep the mail from getting wet.

Most passengers still didn't realize how serious things were. Some third-class passengers had discovered that their deck was covered with ice that had fallen from the iceberg. Some began to have a snowball fight. Soon passengers from every class were picking up pieces of ice. Some even used the ice to cool their drinks. Whatever the problem, they seemed confident that it would soon be solved.

A few passengers, however, were well aware that something was terribly wrong. Lawrence Beasley, a schoolteacher traveling in second class, had started back to his cabin when he noticed that somehow his feet weren't falling in the right place. The stairs were level, but he felt slightly off balance. It was as if the steps were suddenly tilting forward toward the *bow,* the front part of the ship. In fact, they were.

Checking for Damage

Below the decks was Thomas Andrews, the chief engineer who had supervised the design of the *Titanic.* He was on board to see how the ship would perform on her maiden voyage and whether any adjustments needed to be made. No one knew the *Titanic* better than Andrews. No man, not even Captain Smith, commanded more respect from the crew. Now the ship's officers were anxiously waiting for him to tell them what was happening.

Andrews studied the reports of the damage and then gave Captain Smith the bad news: The rock-hard base of the iceberg had scraped the *Titanic*'s hull below the waterline, gashing some holes in her side and loosening the steel plates that held her together. Water was rushing into the front of the ship. Andrews explained there were 16 watertight compartments on the ship from bow to *stern,* the back end of the ship. The ship could float if the first four were filled. But if the fifth compartment, or bulkhead, was filled, the bow would begin to sink so low that water would spill over that bulkhead into the sixth compartment. Because the *Titanic*'s bulkheads were not high enough to prevent this from happening, the spillover would continue from compartment to compartment until the whole ship filled with water and sank.

The *Titanic* was doomed.

"How long have we got?" the captain asked.

"About two hours," Andrews replied.

Smith and Andrews both knew that there were 2,207 passengers and crew on board, but room for only about 1,178 people in the lifeboats. Unless a rescue ship arrived within two hours, more than 1,000 people would drown. There was no time to waste.

SOS

At 12:15 A.M., Captain Smith ordered the radio operator to send out the international distress call. Immediately, a cry for help went out over the dark, cold ocean. The new international signal for distress, SOS, was being used for the first time. Ten miles away, the freighter *Californian* was surrounded by ice. Because the *Californian*'s radio operator had gone to bed, there was no one on duty to hear the *Titanic*'s cry for help.

Meanwhile, on board the *Titanic,* stewards were going from cabin to cabin, crying, "Everybody upstairs! Life belts on." Some of the elderly first-class passengers became confused. The stewards told them to put on two suits of woolen underwear and extra sweaters. Then the stewards tied the elderly passengers' shoelaces and sent them upstairs like children going off to school.

Slowly, people began to stumble onto the deck. Many had been asleep, and they were bewildered and half-dressed. Some women wore fur coats over their thin nightgowns. Some wore just their nightclothes. A few were dressed in summer clothes. But they all wore life preservers.

The big decision for many passengers was what to take and what to leave behind. Major Arthur Kessler was carrying $300,000 worth of stocks and bonds in a metal box. He looked at it for several moments, then quickly grabbed three oranges, put them in his pocket, and left his fortune on the table.

While the first-class and some second-class passengers were led to the lifeboats quickly, third-class passengers were held below for almost an hour. As a result, whole families were lost.

Most crew members knew they wouldn't escape in the lifeboats. Passengers would be selected first. Thirty-four engineers, boiler-room workers, electricians, and plumbers bravely remained below to keep the ship's lights on so that

28

passengers wouldn't have to abandon ship in the dark. The engineers knew they were sentencing themselves to death.

Other crew members also showed a great deal of courage. When the passengers gathered on the decks, they were greeted by a surprising sound: Wallace Hartley, the bandleader, had gathered his eight musicians on deck to play lively jazz tunes. The music created an almost festive air on board and helped prevent widespread panic.

Lowering the Lifeboats

As the lifeboats were lowered, it became clear that most of the crew had no idea of how to use the equipment. They hadn't been properly trained because nobody thought lifeboats would ever be needed on the "unsinkable" ship. As a result, the crew members were poorly organized and unable to handle the crisis. They sent out some boats only one-half or two-thirds full even though there were plenty of passengers standing nearby, waiting to board.

Many of the passengers were actually reluctant to enter the lifeboats at first. They didn't believe they really were in danger. "I was told that God Himself couldn't sink this ship," one woman complained. Others felt that even if the *Titanic* was sinking, there was still enough time for rescue ships to arrive. They thought they would be safer on board than in a lifeboat. But some passengers had already noticed that the ship was beginning to tilt slightly forward and to the side—a sign that it was filling up with water.

"Women and children first," the ship's officers cried out. And finally, with great hesitation, women and children began entering the lifeboats.

Despite their lack of training, the crew prepared the lifeboats as quickly as they could. Fifth Officer Harold Lowe was a tough, experienced sailor who did his job well and knew his own mind. As he was slowly lowering a lifeboat filled with passengers, Bruce Ismay, the owner of the ship, shouted at him to go faster. Lowe angrily shouted back: "If you get . . . out of my way, I'll be able to do something. You'll have me drown the whole lot of them." The other crew members were shocked to hear Lowe talking to the owner that way. But Ismay kept quiet and walked away. He knew Lowe would do his best job if he were left alone.

Boarding the lifeboats was the most difficult moment for the passengers. According to maritime custom, women and children evacuated the ship first. Husbands had to convince their wives to leave without them—often for the sake of their children. People believed that a man must always act with dignity and consideration in an emergency, even if it cost him his life. Families separated. Children cried as they were lowered into the lifeboats while their fathers stood on the deck and waved good-bye. Husbands and wives embraced and kissed for the last time. Colonel Astor

The men say a final good-bye to their wives and children.

asked if he could accompany his pregnant young wife, but he was refused by one of the officers who did not know who Astor was. The famous millionaire stood on the deck and casually smoked a cigarette as his wife was lowered in the boat. "I'll be on the next one," he called out, then waved good-bye with a smile. He never saw his wife again.

Walter Douglas's wife insisted, "Walter, you must come with me." He replied, "No, I must be a gentleman." Other men assured their wives and children that they would come later or that a rescue ship was on its way and would arrive soon, even if they really didn't believe it. Charles Guggenheim refused to go until all the women and children were off the ship. "Tell my wife I've done my best in doing my duty," he said. He and his valet then went to his cabin. The two of them put on evening clothes and returned to the deck. "We've dressed our best and are prepared to go down like gentleman."

Some wives and children absolutely refused to be parted from their husbands. Mrs. Hudson Allison of Montreal and her daughter Lorraine stayed behind with Mr. Allison. When Isidor Straus, the elderly owner of Macy's, was offered a seat on the lifeboat because of his age, he refused. "I'll wait with the other men," he replied. His wife Ida then refused to go without him. "I've always stayed with my husband. Why should I leave him now?" Hand in hand they walked onto the deck and sat down in lounge chairs. Michael Navratil, the man who had kidnapped his two small children from his wife, escorted them to a lifeboat and then handed them over to an officer. He remained on board.

The policy of women and children leaving first wasn't always practical, however, and exceptions were made. Men, especially crew members, were needed to row the boats. A few newlywed husbands were allowed to go with their wives. Some men got into the lifeboats because there

31

were no women or children immediately around. Some jumped into the boats as they were being lowered, and a few managed to hide in the vessels. One man was accused of dressing in woman's clothing in order to get into a lifeboat, but there was no evidence to support this charge.

Several men and boys were forced at gunpoint by the ship's officers to climb out of boats they had entered. Any male over eight years of age was considered a man, although once again exceptions were made. A number of crewmen jumped into boats. One man who saved himself was the owner of the ship, Bruce Ismay. Even though he seemed to have a perfectly good reason to leave—there were no other passengers immediately available to board when a lifeboat was being lowered—his escape ruined his reputation for the rest of his life. Many people blamed him for the disaster and thought he should have gone down with his ship.

Because most of the lifeboats were lowered while only

This photograph of Titanic *survivors aboard a lifeboat was taken by one of the few ships that came to the rescue of the* Titanic.

partially full, almost 500 people who could have been saved were not. In the worst case, a lifeboat that was built to hold more than 60 people was lowered with only 12 aboard, and most of those were crew. Among the few passengers aboard were Sir Cosmo and Lady Duff Gordon, an English nobleman and his wife, who were traveling first class.

Second- and especially third-class passengers received little help in finding boats. Even when the stewards tried to assist them, many of the immigrants didn't speak English and didn't understand what was going on. A few bold third-class passengers made their way up to the decks and onto a lifeboat. But many others simply gathered around a priest and began to pray or prepare themselves for death.

Other people tried to entertain themselves while they waited for the end. A few played cards in the lounge even though the surfaces of the tables were now at an angle. As the boat continued to sink, the bartender served free drinks. The gym instructor showed a number of people how to use some of the new gym equipment. And the band played on.

Meanwhile, the *Titanic*'s distress signals were being picked up by ships from a variety of countries. The closest was the *Carpathia,* a British ship, but she was 50 miles away and her speed was a slow 14 knots an hour. At that rate, it would take her almost four hours to arrive. The *Titanic* would sink in less than two.

The only ship nearby that could have saved the *Titanic*'s passengers and crew was the *Californian,* which was less than 30 minutes away. The crews of both ships could see each other's lights. Yet no one on the *Californian* even realized that the *Titanic* was in trouble. When the *Californian*'s crew spotted the sinking ship's blinking SOS signal, they assumed it was just a bobbing light from the *Titanic*'s mast. They ignored it.

In desperation, the *Titanic* sent up rocket flares to signal her distress. A crew member of the *Californian* finally woke Captain Stanley Lord to tell him about the flares. But instead of trying to reach the *Titanic* by radio, Captain Lord told his men to try and signal the ship by Morse light. When there was no response to the signal (it wasn't seen clearly by those aboard the *Titanic*), the captain went back to sleep.

By 2:05 A.M., the last lifeboat had departed the *Titanic.* The *Carpathia,* steaming to the rescue, was now three hours away. But the *Titanic,* with almost 1,500 people still on board, had only 15 minutes left.

5

The End of the *Titanic*

Those still on board the *Titanic* quietly watched the lifeboats depart. A sudden calm settled over the sinking ship. Some say the band continued to play almost to the end. Many third-class passengers finally managed to reach the deck only to find that there were no more lifeboats left.

As the front end of the ship continued to slip deeper into the ocean and water crept higher over the deck, the remaining passengers rushed toward the rear. They thought that if they could only get to the stern, somehow they would be spared. One woman cried out to a steward, "Save me! Save me!" He replied, "Only God can save you now."

Not everyone panicked. William Stead, a writer, read in the library. Thomas Andrews, the ship's chief engineer, sat staring at a wall in the lounge. He and Captain Smith had decided to go down with the ship. One woman played a piano, her child on her lap. The ship's chief baker, Charles Joughin, thought he had the best solution—alcohol. He worked hard helping passengers board the lifeboats, then dashed to his cabin for several drinks before returning to help others. When the last lifeboat was gone, Joughin began tossing deck chairs overboard so that those who managed to survive in the water would have something to hold on to. As the *Titanic* neared its end, Joughin was prepared to die.

By 2:10 A.M. the bow of the ship was deep in the water and its stern was high in the air.

Desperate Measures

A few passengers and crew members chose to dive into the ocean rather than be dragged down by the sinking ship. Two friends, Jack Thayer and Milton Long, decided to jump together. Long slid down the side of the ship while Thayer jumped out as far as he could. Thayer made it and was saved, but Long drowned.

First Officer Charles Lightoller dived headfirst into the sea. Immediately dragged down by water rushing into one of the ship's air vents, he was pinned against the grating. In another few moments he would have been pulled through the vent and sucked down into the ship. But a burst of hot air from deep inside the boiler room suddenly shot up through the vent and pushed him safely to the surface. Now the task Lightoller and the others faced in the ice-cold water was to keep from freezing to death.

The ship was now sticking almost straight up in the air. Passengers on deck could no longer stand. They were shouting "Good-bye" and "I love you." From the water, Jack Thayer saw people slide off the deck and into the ocean. "We could see groups of people . . . in . . . bunches, like swarming bees, only to fall in masses, pairs, or singly as the great part of the ship . . . rose into the sky."

A rumbling noise was heard inside the ship as all movable objects began to slide forward—chairs, tables, plates, glasses, pianos, beds, and bureaus. Then there was an even greater crash as the ship's boilers, furnaces, and heavy machinery tore loose and rolled toward the front of the ship. The lights went out, and with a roar the *Titanic* began to sink into the waves. The ship, according to many, began to break in two.

Standing on the outside of the stern was Chief Baker Joughin, alert but relaxed from the drinking he had done. Like a man on an elevator, Joughin calmly rode the *Titanic* 150 feet down toward the sea. As the end of the ship reached the waves, he calmly stepped off and into the ocean. Once he was swimming, Joughin found that instead of freezing, he hardly felt the cold. He was able to survive the cold because he couldn't feel it. He managed to stay alive until he was rescued.

Rose Abbot, a third-class passenger who had stayed on the ship when it went down, miraculously escaped. Earlier, she had refused to board a lifeboat without her two sons who were too old to be considered children. Now she was prepared to die with them. Down she plunged, holding her boys tightly against her. Almost immediately, the children were torn out of her arms by the swirling water. But then as pieces of wood suddenly began shooting up to the surface, Rose Abbot found herself trapped among them. The wood almost battered her to death, but it also carried her along to the surface. She was spared.

For the almost 1,500 others who had been left on board, however, there were no miracles. When they hit the water, some people were crushed to death by one of the ship's smokestacks. For those who actually went down with the ship, the end was quick. Within seconds, their lungs burst under the pressure of the water. In a way, they were the lucky ones. The greatest agony was suffered by those who survived the sinking, only to find themselves in the cold, dark ocean.

The water was 28 degrees Farenheit—4 degrees below freezing. The cold was so intense it cut through people like a knife. After the initial shock wore off, hundreds of people began to swim around, looking for something or someone to keep them afloat. People grabbed one another, often drowning themselves and those they were holding onto. Some clung to pieces of wood, chairs, or doors that had been thrown into the sea.

A few of the swimmers were lucky. Officer Lightoller, Jack Thayer, and several others who jumped off the ship found two of the smaller lifeboats floating in the water. The crew had been unable to loosen the boats earlier. Now the boats were thrown free by the sinking ship. One was upside down, and people had to scramble up onto the bottom of the boat. Radio operator Harold Bridge struggled underneath one of the boats before he managed to get on board. Lightoller was also able to climb on, and so was Thayer. Soon the boat was packed with too many people. When still another swimmer tried to board, a passenger cried out, "One more would sink us all."

The swimmer didn't argue. "Good luck," he called out. "God bless you." And then he swam away. Some thought the man was Captain Smith.

But for most people in the water, the experience was a nightmare. They began to groan with pain, howling and crying for help, begging to be saved. Their voices blended together in a low roar that spread over the surface of the frigid sea. As 12-year-old Ruth Becker, who had been lowered into a lifeboat, remembered: "There fell upon the ear the most terrible noise human beings ever listened to . . . the cries of hundreds of people struggling in the ice-cold water, crying for help with a cry that we knew could not be answered."

There were hundreds of people swimming in the water— and there was enough room in the lifeboats for all of them. But only Officer Harold Lowe went back deliberately to pick up survivors. In some boats the officers would have turned back, but the passengers refused, rescuing only survivors swimming conveniently close by. "Why should we lose our lives, when we can't help them?" Sir Cosmo Duff Gordon remarked. His boat, which could hold 60 people, had only 12 on board.

Fights broke out in some other boats over that same question. By the time the arguments were over, it was too late. Those in the water had stopped crying for help. Their life jackets couldn't protect them against the bitter cold. They had either frozen to death or drowned. The 18 lifeboats now at sea had rescued only 13 drowning people, almost half of them by one boat alone—Officer Lowe's.

Throughout the night, the people in the lifeboats did their best to keep warm. Rowing helped, and in most boats men and women shared the burden equally. In a few boats, the women took charge because the men were either too drunk or too frightened to be of use. As the night dragged on, a few people lost consciousness, slipped into comas, and died. Unless help arrived soon, more would join them.

The *Carpathia*

Meanwhile, the *Carpathia* was steaming to the rescue. Its captain, Arthur Rostow, was a man of action. His crew called him "The Electric Spark" because he was so quick to act in an emergency. While Captain Stanley Lord continued to sleep soundly aboard the *Californian* only 30 minutes away from the lifeboats, Captain Rostow was pushing the *Carpathia* as fast as it could go in a desperate attempt to rescue anyone who may have survived. He ordered the engine room to push the ship to 17 knots, risking a boiler explosion in the process. Rostow then prepared his ship to receive survivors. Lounges were turned into hospital rooms. Blankets and clothing were gathered. Gallons of coffee and soup were heated. Doctors and nurses were organized to take care of patients.

At 3:30 A.M., the *Carpathia*'s lookout spotted a dark

shape in the water. At first, he thought it was the *Titanic,* but it turned out to be an iceberg. The *Carpathia* was now entering the same icefield that the *Titanic* had sailed through. But unlike Captain Smith, Rostow had posted lookouts almost everywhere on the ship. As a result, the *Carpathia* was able to avoid the deadly ice.

As dawn approached, the crew on the *Carpathia* spotted bright green flares in the distance. Captain Rostow hoped they were coming from the *Titanic,* but they were from the lifeboats. When the *Carpathia* picked up the first boatload of survivors, Rostow's worst fear was confirmed: The *Titanic* had sunk to the bottom of the ocean, taking most of those on board with her.

During the next several hours, the *Carpathia* rescued all

Survivors of the Titanic *warm themselves after being rescued by the* Carpathia.

the passengers in the lifeboats. Approximately 700 out of the 2,207 people who had sailed on the *Titanic* were saved. Once on board the *Carpathia,* some families happily discovered relatives they thought had perished. But almost everyone lost someone—a husband, wife, mother, father, child, sister, brother, or friend. Although the *Carpathia* continued to search for hours, no survivors were found floating in the water.

The *Carpathia* was still searching when Captain Lord of the *Californian* finally decided to wake up his radio operator to find out if anything had happened during the night. Lord soon discovered that he had slept through the sinking of the *Titanic.* He then asked the *Carpathia* what he could do to help and was told by an angry Captain Rostow that he could go search for the dead.

The Investigation

As soon as the shocking news of the *Titanic*'s sinking reached the United States and Britain, people demanded information. They wanted to know what had happened and who was to blame. Both the United States and Britain held their own investigations. The two sides bitterly criticized each other, yet they basically reached the same conclusions.

Both countries believed that the *Titanic* hadn't been prepared properly for a voyage through the icefields. Both blamed the British Board of Trade for not requiring the *Titanic* to have enough lifeboats. They agreed that the crew was poorly trained to man the lifeboats and poorly organized when the emergency arose. Both Britain and the United States raised serious questions about why the passengers and crew in the lifeboats hadn't stopped to rescue survivors. The Americans especially criticized the White Star Line for the *Titanic*'s unsafe design.

Because he died a hero's death, the Americans only

The New York Times.

THE WEATHER

VOL. LXI...NO. 19,886.

NEW YORK, TUESDAY, APRIL 16, 1912.—TWENTY-FOUR PAGES.

ONE CENT

TITANIC SINKS FOUR HOURS AFTER HITTING ICEBERG;
866 RESCUED BY CARPATHIA, PROBABLY 1250 PERISH;
ISMAY SAFE, MRS. ASTOR MAYBE, NOTED NAMES MISSING

Col. Astor and Bride, Isidor Straus and Wife, and Maj. Butt Aboard.

"RULE OF SEA" FOLLOWED

Women and Children Put Over in Lifeboats and Supposed to be Safe on Carpathia.

PICKED UP AFTER 8 HOURS

Vincent Astor Calls at White Star Office for News of His Father and Leaves Weeping.

FRANKLIN HOPEFUL ALL DAY

Manager of the Line Insisted Titanic Was Unsinkable Even After She Had Gone Down.

HEAD OF THE LINE ABOARD

J. Bruce Ismay Making First Trip on Gigantic Ship That Was to Surpass All Others.

Biggest Liner Plunges to the Bottom at 2:20 A. M.

RESCUERS THERE TOO LATE

Except to Pick Up the Few Hundreds Who Took to the Lifeboats.

WOMEN AND CHILDREN FIRST

Cunarder Carpathia Rushing to New York with the Survivors.

SEA SEARCH FOR OTHERS

The California Stands By on Chance of Picking Up Other Boats or Rafts.

OLYMPIC SENDS THE NEWS

Only Ship to Flash Wireless Messages to Shore After the Disaster.

The Lost Titanic Being Towed Out of Belfast Harbor.

PARTIAL LIST OF THE SAVED.

Includes Bruce Ismay, Mrs. Widener, Mrs. H. B. Harris, and an Incomplete name, suggesting Mrs. Astor's.

CAPT. E. J. SMITH,
Commander of the Titanic.

The sinking of the Titanic *made front-page news around the world.*

mildly criticized Captain Smith, and the British were unwilling to criticize him at all. Yet it is clear that Smith showed poor judgment by not slowing down while traveling near icebergs. Captain Stanley Lord of the *Californian* was severely criticized but not punished for his failure to respond to the *Titanic*'s distress signals. Although Captain Lord insisted that he had been trapped in an icefield and therefore couldn't have helped the *Titanic* without endangering his own ship, both investigating committees concluded that he could have saved the passengers and crew. For the rest of his life, Captain Lord lived in disgrace.

Another person disgraced by the tragedy was Bruce Ismay, the ship owner who saved his own life when so many others died. Many believed he should have made sure that all the women and children were safe before he left the ship. Although Ismay was cleared of acting improperly, he resigned from the company and was rarely seen again in public.

One question that neither investigating committee looked at too closely was whether the first-class passengers were put onto the lifeboats ahead of those in second and third class. The official answer was no, but the statistics tell a different story.

All the first-class children and most of the first-class women survived. The few exceptions were those whose families chose to stay on board rather than be separated from their husbands and children. All second-class children were saved as well, and so were 80 of the 93 second-class women. But out of 79 children and 165 women in third class, 52 children and 89 women died. That is almost two-thirds of the children and more than half of the women.

Although many of the men on board drowned, again there were great differences according to class. Out of 118 first-class men, 57 were saved. But only 14 of the 168 second-class men survived, and only 75 out of 462 third-class men. Of the crew, only 212 out of almost 900 survived.

Were second- and third-class passengers held back to save those in first class? The answer appears to be yes. Although no specific orders were given, it is clear that most crew members felt their greatest responsibility was to save the first-class passengers.

As a result of the tragedy, Britain and the United States took measures to prevent another disaster like the sinking of the *Titanic*. The number of lifeboats was increased on all ships—enough for every passenger in every class. Laws were passed requiring every oceangoing ship to have radio operators on duty 24 hours a day. An international ice patrol was organized to warn ships of icebergs. Sea routes were changed to avoid the most dangerous areas. And ships were redesigned to make them stronger and less likely to be damaged by collisions at sea. Had any one of these precautions been taken earlier, the tragedy of the *Titanic* might never have happened.

6

In Search of the *Titanic*

When the *Titanic* sank, she came to rest about 12,500 feet beneath the sea. There was not a man or woman alive who knew exactly where the remains of the great ship lay. Even after the *Titanic* no longer made headlines, many people dreamed of finding her. The first were the relatives of three of the wealthiest victims—the Astors, Guggenheims, and Wideners. Shortly after the sinking, they contacted a company that specialized in bringing up wrecked ships from the bottom of the ocean and asked if the *Titanic* could be recovered. The answer was no. It wasn't until 1986 that the lost ship was found.

Dreams and Schemes

For 74 years the *Titanic* lay undisturbed on the ocean floor. During that time people came up with highly imaginative—and often highly unscientific—schemes to find the ship and bring it to the surface. These weren't practical ideas—after all, no one knew the exact location of the ship, so they couldn't very well bring it to the surface. Stories about these schemes appeared periodically in newspapers, as many as 40 years after the sinking.

In 1914, Charles Smith, an American architect, suggested building a special submarine with powerful magnets that would be attracted to the *Titanic*'s side. Once the sunken ship was located, more magnets would be attached to it. The magnets and the *Titanic* would then be pulled to the surface by giant cables.

Others had even stranger ideas. During the 1970s, one inventor suggested that the *Titanic*'s interior be filled with Ping-Pong balls to make the ship float to the surface. Another person had a similar plan but would use balloons instead. A third man suggested wrapping the ship in ice created by freezing nitrogen gas. Since ice is lighter than water, he was convinced that the ship would float to the surface inside the huge ice cube. Still another man wanted to fill the *Titanic* with 180,000 tons of wax which he claimed would rise to the water's surface when it hardened, lifting the ship with it.

1967 was the year that the first really serious hope came along for a *Titanic* recovery. That year a young marine scientist named Robert Ballard attended a meeting of the Boston Sea Rovers, a group of sea lovers. The topic of discussion was the dream of every underwater explorer—the dream of recovering the *Titanic*. Ballard listened eagerly. He had been assigned to the U.S. Navy's Deep Submergence Group at the Woods Hole Oceanographic Institute in Woods Hole, Massachusetts, and his specialty was deep-sea diving.

Ballard had been fascinated by the sea ever since he was a child, collecting shells and driftwood along the California coast where he grew up. When he was a teenager, Ballard realized that he was more interested in scuba diving than surfing with his friends. His favorite book was Jules Verne's *20,000 Leagues Under the Sea,* a fantasy about a sea captain who lived underwater in his submarine, the *Nautilus.*

Ballard studied marine geology in college, working with robots designed for underwater exploration. In 1973 the Navy assigned Ballard to *Alvin,* a submarine for oceanic exploration operated by a three-man crew.

Alvin could dive to a depth of only 6,000 feet. But in the 1970s, the Navy rebuilt *Alvin* with a new hull made of titanium, which was strong enough to withstand pressures as far down as 13,000 feet underwater. Suddenly, it occurred to Ballard that since the *Titanic* lay about 12,500 feet below the surface, *Alvin* could be used to find her. For the next 12 years, he desperately tried to raise the money he needed to do the job.

In 1980, however, Ballard began to worry that someone else might beat him to it. A Texas oil millionaire, Jack Grimm, was planning to search for the *Titanic*. Grimm was known as "Cadillac Jack" because he loved to collect Cadillac cars.

Grimm's scientists first searched the area where one of the *Titanic*'s officers thought the ship had sunk, but they were unable to locate it. On their second attempt, Grimm insisted that the crew take a monkey on board their research vessel. He believed that the monkey could point to a spot on the map and the *Titanic* would be found there. The scientists refused to base their search on a monkey—or a Texas millionaire. So they told Grimm that he had a choice —the monkey or them. Grimm finally gave up, and the ship sailed without the monkey. But despite several promising leads, the crew had no success this time either. In 1983, Grimm made one more attempt to find the *Titanic*, but he failed again.

While Grimm's scientists were searching for the *Titanic*, Ballard was developing a unique robot video camera system that could take pictures at the bottom of the sea. About the size of an automobile, the system was equipped with five cameras, sonar and other sensing devices, and powerful lights. (*Sonar* is a system that sends out sound waves to locate objects. When the sound waves strike something, they bounce back—like a ball bouncing off a wall—and the returning waves are recorded on a scope.) A boat on the surface of the water could control the robot camera while it explored the depths of the sea.

Ballard called the system *Argo,* after a ship sailed by the Greek mythological hero Jason. Before Jason could marry a beautiful princess, he first had to sail around the world and bring back a sheep's fleece made of gold. After many adventures in his ship, called the *Argo,* Jason managed to find—and bring back—the fleece. Ballard hoped the name *Argo* would bring him good luck in his own search.

Ballard's Search

By 1985, Ballard was ready to begin. He loaded *Argo* and another photographic-sonar system, ANGUS, on his re-

Dr. Robert Ballard (second from right) shakes hands with Jean-Louis Michel (far right) aboard his research ship, the Knorr, *in 1985. Argo, Ballard's robot video camera system, is directly behind the crew.*

search ship, the *Knorr*. Part of the funding for his search came from the Navy, which was interested in Ballard's underwater equipment. To raise the rest of the money, Ballard joined forces with the French Oceanographic Institute. The leader of the Institute was Jean-Louis Michel, an old friend of Ballard's.

The French-American team planned to carry out their search in two steps. First, the French hoped to locate the *Titanic* by scanning a 150-square-mile area with a highly developed sonar system called SAR. If they found the ship, Ballard would then lower his video system to take pictures. If they didn't find it, Ballard would continue the search with *Argo*.

Summertime was considered the best season to work in the ocean since there were usually few storms. Also, they had only five weeks to complete their mission because both boats would then be needed elsewhere. So on July 1, 1985, the French and American teams boarded the French research vessel, *Le Suroit*. The sonar system was lowered from the boat by cable, more than 12,000 feet down to the ocean floor. Then the search began.

Day after day, the crew searched the chosen area, a process oceanographers called "mowing the lawn" because the sonar sweeps over the ocean floor like a lawn mower. In five weeks they covered almost 80 percent of the area without finding any sign of the *Titanic*. Part of the problem was that unseasonal storms and strong ocean currents kept pulling their boat off course.

After *Le Suroit* returned home, it was Ballard's turn to explore the rest of the area. He and his crew and Jean-Louis Michel boarded the *Knorr* and went in search of the *Titanic*. Ballard realized that the odds were against their locating a ship in hundreds of square miles of water 2½ miles below the surface. It would have been easier to find a needle in a haystack. Not only was Ballard uncertain about where the ship was, but he didn't even know if it was still resting on the ocean floor. It could have been buried in mud—or covered up by an earthquake. It might even have broken up completely when it hit the bottom.

Ballard planned to start with a 30-square-mile area that hadn't yet been searched. Like the French sonar, *Argo* would be lowered to a depth of more than 12,000 feet, just above the ocean floor. Then Ballard would slowly tow *Argo* close to the bottom so that its five cameras could scan the area. Ballard and his crew would watch *Argo*'s pictures on video screens in the *Knorr*'s control room.

Ballard reasoned that as the *Titanic* sank, all sorts of objects must have fallen out of the ship. The debris would have scattered over the ocean floor. Ballard was hoping to spot some of these objects and then follow their trail to the ship.

On August 25, 1985, the search began. As Ballard and his men watched on the *Knorr, Argo*'s television cameras began sending back pictures.

Day after day, the *Knorr* moved slowly across the ocean, dragging *Argo* along. For 24 hours a day, in 4-hour shifts, the crew sat with their eyes fixed on the TV monitor. All they saw was miles and miles of ocean mud and sand dunes. A few rat-tailed fish occasionally swam across the screen. However, it was rare to see living creatures because most fish cannot withstand the enormous pressure of the water at such great depths.

The crew was becoming bored and restless. Most of them ate large amounts of popcorn, and some smoked constantly. As time was running out, Ballard decided to scan a small area that the French sonar team had missed because of strong currents. It was his last hope.

The search produced no immediate results. The tension on the ship was becoming almost unbearable. Only four days were left to go. At midnight on August 30, Jean-Louis Michel's crew took over as usual for the early-morning shift. Billy Lange and Stu Harris were assigned to watch the television screen. Shortly before 1:00 A.M., they were joking about what they could do to keep from falling asleep, when Billy suddenly pointed to the screen and cried, "There's something!"

Stu turned to look. Seconds passed, and then Billy exclaimed, "It's coming in. Wreckage!"

"Bingo!" Stu shot back.

Everybody gathered around. The men shouted and cheered as the camera drifted by a number of objects. A large, round shape turned out to be one of the *Titanic*'s boilers. After 73 years, the first clue to the *Titanic*'s location had been discovered about 1,200 miles from the dock at Southampton in southern England.

The men couldn't tear themselves away to go get Ballard, who was in his cabin. Finally, the cook was instructed to give him the news. Minutes later, Ballard rushed into the video control center. He stared wide-eyed as wreckage from the *Titanic* appeared before him. A piece of railing . . . a porthole . . . then, out of the gloom, the ship's deck came into view. The *Titanic* had been found!

At around 2:00 A.M., Ballard remembered that it was about this hour that the *Titanic* had sunk. He thought of all those who had lost their lives here. Ballard led the crew out onto the deck for a silent memorial service to pay tribute to them. The sky was filled with stars and the ocean was calm. Except for the presence of the moon and the absence of cold, it was very much like the night the *Titanic* sank.

Ballard decided to make several passes over the sunken ship. The crew watched with great excitement as the camera descended toward its target. And suddenly, there it

51

was, sitting upright in the mud, in seemingly excellent condition. *Argo* had located the *Titanic*'s bow, the front part of the ship. The stern, however, was missing. It was later discovered 2,000 feet away.

Just then, the weather turned bad and Ballard decided it would be dangerous to leave *Argo* below. He decided to use ANGUS to take detailed still photographs. Since *Argo* had taken only black-and-white video images from a distance, the photos in the first group were fuzzy and disappointing. Despite the risk that the unit might get caught in the wreckage, Ballard then lowered ANGUS to within a few yards of the *Titanic*. This time luck was on his side.

The photographs showed that there was a giant hole where a funnel had been, but the anchors were still locked

This picture of a safe with its bottom blown out was taken near the Titanic *by a photographic-sonar system called ANGUS.*

in place on the sides of the ship. There were many wine bottles, unbroken and still corked. The crow's nest from which Frederick Fleet had first spotted the iceberg was still attached to the mast. There was luggage all around, as well as a silver platter and even a safe with its bottom blown out.

Ballard was still worried about the equipment getting damaged, so he reluctantly headed for home. He knew it would be easy to return to the *Titanic* for further exploration. But it would be hard to keep the ship's location a secret until his work was finished.

Back in the United States, Ballard was given a hero's welcome. Hundreds of boats, planes, and helicopters came out to greet him, and thousands of cheering people lined the dock. He was interviewed by the press and appeared on television, expressing his hope that the *Titanic* would be left in peace. All he wanted was to go back and explore her without disturbing the ship.

Ballard "Boards" the *Titanic*

In the summer of 1986, Ballard was ready to get a closer look at the *Titanic*. This time, he sailed on the research vessel *Atlantis II* with two new pieces of equipment. One was a hi-tech mobile camera unit, controlled and powered through a 250-foot cable. Known as *Jason Jr.,* or *JJ,* it could move around in tight places and even enter the sunken ship. It carried video and still cameras as well as powerful light sources.

To explore the ocean floor, *JJ* needed to hitch a ride. The vehicle that would carry the robot down was *Alvin,* the small submarine Ballard had thought of using in his search for the *Titanic* while he was still in the Navy. With *JJ* attached to *Alvin's* back, *Alvin* could take the mobile camera and the three-man crew to the bottom of the ocean.

On the morning of July 13, Ballard and his two pilots squeezed into *Alvin*. As the submarine slowly descended, it passed from brightness to gloom to total darkness. At 1,200 feet below the surface, the crew reached the depth that daylight cannot penetrate. Though the submarine had electrically powered lights, Ballard didn't want to waste the batteries. He wanted to save power for the *Titanic*.

During *Alvin*'s descent, the crew played classical music and ate peanut-butter sandwiches. At 2,000 feet, *Alvin* passed through a layer of sea life that looked like a cloudy blur on the sonar screen. This "cloud" was made up of tens of thousands of tiny creatures, many of which glowed in the dark. As the submarine passed through the mass of ocean creatures, they lit up like tiny fireworks.

At 5,000 feet, it became cold inside the submarine and the crew put on extra clothing. They were getting cramped and tired from sitting in one position without moving. As they continued their descent, the instrument panel showed that salt water was leaking into one of the batteries. Their time on the bottom would have to be limited.

Finally, *Alvin* reached the ocean floor and Ballard turned on its lights to look for the *Titanic*. A few minutes later, an alarm suddenly shrieked through the submarine. Sea water had reached *Alvin*'s batteries and the sub was in danger of losing its power. The pressure at that depth was great—6,000 pounds per square inch. Ballard and his pilots had only a few minutes in which to begin surfacing. To make matters worse, their sonar had stopped working. Their only hope of sighting the ship was by looking through *Alvin*'s window. It seemed an impossible task. But suddenly they saw in front of them a towering black wall of rusted steel rising out of the mud and extending high above them. The *Titanic!* That one glimpse was all they got. They had to begin their return to the surface immediately or run the risk of remaining below forever. For the next 2½ hours, the three frustrated scientists rode to the surface while listening to soft rock music on their stereo system.

But Ballard refused to give up. The batteries were quickly repaired and *Alvin* returned to the bottom of the sea. For the next 11 days, Ballard and his crew explored the *Titanic*. They discovered that wood-boring worms had eaten almost every trace of wood on the ship. The deck was gone, along with the interior paneling and the famous grand staircase. The steel plate inside and out was rusted, but the motion of the currents had polished all the brass, copper, and bronze objects on the ship, making them look shiny and new.

One of the great moments of their exploration came when *JJ*—the swimming eyeball—was successfully sent inside the sunken ship. The video robot entered places that were too dangerous or too small for *Alvin*. *JJ* photographed the grand ballroom and other areas. Amid the destruction, Ballard was amazed to find that a chandelier had survived the 2½ mile fall with its light sockets in place.

Ballard didn't expect to find the remains of any of the victims, but as he was photographing a number of objects that had fallen onto the ocean floor—pots, pans, dishes, wine bottles, chairs, faucets—he was startled to see a smiling child-like face looking up at him from the muddy bottom. It turned out to be a doll's head. Though no human remains were actually discovered, every once in a while the submarine would pass over a pair of shoes positioned in the mud in such a way that Ballard was sure a person had once been lying in them.

Ballard and his crew had hoped to discover just why the *Titanic* sank. But her bow was buried 60 feet in the sand. They could see that the seams of the steel plates holding the ship together had been sprung, but they couldn't tell

Jason Jr. photographed a chandelier on the ocean floor with its light sockets still in place, but with some coral growing out of its side!

whether this damage was caused by the iceberg or the fall to the ocean floor.

As he explored the *Titanic,* Ballard again and again thought of the men and women and children who had gone down with her. He had written a memorial plaque to leave on the deck of the stern, the place where so many people had gathered for safety just before the ship went down. The plaque was attached to the side of *Alvin,* to be removed by one of its mechanical arms and gently dropped to the *Titanic*'s deck.

By the time Ballard finished his work, *Alvin* and *JJ* had made 11 trips, and had taken more than 50,000 still pictures and 100 hours of videotape. Although he could easily have done so, Ballard took no souvenirs with him. He wanted to let the *Titanic* rest in peace.

Not everyone agreed. Immediately after Ballard's discovery, Jack Grimm, the Texas oil millionaire, paid the French Oceanographic Institute to bring back some debris from the ship in 1987. It is now on exhibit in France.

In 1991 a Canadian-Russian-American team returned to the *Titanic* with super-bright lights to take more pictures. During the dive, Emory Kristof, a photographer for *National Geographic* magazine, made a three-dimensional movie of the wreck called *Titanica*. The film will be shown in museums and aquariums.

A number of companies are currently competing for the chance to salvage the *Titanic,* and the courts are determining who has the rights to the ship. It's a complicated question because the *Titanic* lies in international waters. That means no one country can claim control of the underwater area on which the ship rests. Perhaps the issue will one day be decided in a world court or by the United Nations. The French have retrieved some of the articles from the wreckage. Someday someone may retrieve more of the articles that fell off the ship or are still inside.

It is doubtful, however, that the *Titanic* itself will ever be raised because it is so deeply buried in the mud.

Robert Ballard objects to the *Titanic* being raided by people seeking to make a profit from the tragedy. He would like the ship to remain undisturbed as a memorial to those who died there. He expressed this wish in a report he made shortly after he first sighted the ship:

> The *Titanic* itself lies in 13,000 feet of water on a gently sloping alpine-like countryside overlooking a small canyon below.
>
> Its bow faces north and the ship sits upright on the bottom, its mighty stacks pointing upward.
>
> There is no light at this great depth and little life can be found.

It is quiet and peaceful and a fitting place for the remains of this greatest of sea tragedies to rest.

May it forever remain that way and may God bless these found souls.

Other titles in the Explorer Books series